A Suit of Nettles

A Suit of Nettles

JAMES REANEY

Thirteen original engravings
by Jim Westergard

The Porcupine's Quill

Library and Archives Canada Cataloguing in Publication

Reaney, James, 1926–2008
A suit of nettles / James Reaney; illustrated with thirteen original engravings by Jim Westergard. – 3rd ed.

ISBN 978-0-88984-330-1

I. Title.

PS8535.E24S84 2010 C811'.54 C2009-906354-9

1 2 3 4 • 13 12 11 10

Published by The Porcupine's Quill, 68 Main Street, PO Box 160, Erin, Ontario NOB 1TO. http://porcupinesquill.ca

Represented in Canada by the Literary Press Group.
Trade orders are available from University of Toronto Press.

We acknowledge the support of the Ontario Arts Council and the Canada Council for the Arts for our publishing program. The financial support of the Government of Canada through the Book Publishing Industry Development Program is also gratefully acknowledged. Thanks, also, to the Government of Ontario through the Ontario Media Development Corporation's Ontario Book Initiative.

Canada

ONTARIO ARTS COUNCIL
CONSEIL DES ARTS DE L'ONTARIO

Canada Council for the Arts
Conseil des Arts du Canada

for R.M.S.

A

GOOSE: *Welsh,* gwyz; *Danish,* gaas; *Saxon,* gos; *Russian,* gus; *Latin,* anser; *Greek,* χήυ; *Sanskrit,* haṅsá; *Italian,* oca; *German,* die Gans; *French,* l'oie; *Spanish,* ganso; a general name for the large web-footed birds of the subfamily Anserinae, usually larger than a duck, and smaller than a swan.

B

Old Mother Goose,
When she wanted to wander,
Would ride through the air
On a very fine gander.

C

Gray goose and gander,
  Waft your wings together,
And carry the good king's daughter
  Over the one-strand river.

D

Goosey Goosey Gander where shall we wander …

E

The devil damn thee black, thou cream-faced loon!
Where gott'st thou that goose look? – *Macbeth*

F

Let there be gall enough in thy ink, though thou write with a goose-pen, no matter. – *Twelfth Night*

G

Now tall Agrippa lived close by –
So tall, he almost touch'd the sky;
He had a mighty inkstand, too,
In which a great goose-feather grew. – *Struwwelpeter*

H

What a goose you are. In the Egyptian hieroglyphics the emblem of a vain silly fellow is a goose.

I

The coat of arms of the Company of Musicians – viz., a swan, with expanded wings, within a double tressure [the gridiron], counter, flory, argent. Perverted into a goose striking the bars of a gridiron with its foot, and called 'The Swan and Harp', or 'Goose and Gridiron'.

J

In the times of popery here were no less than eighteen houses on the Bankside, licensed by the Bishops of Winchester … to keep whores, who were, therefore, commonly called Winchester Geese.

K

> For good society is but a game, 'The royal game of Goose', as I may say. – Byron

L

> Galen might goe *shooe the Gander* for any good he could doo…. – Nashe

M

Christmas is a-comin' and the geese are getting fat.

N & ETC.

I wish, gentlemen, it was one of the geese of Ferrara, so much celebrated among the ancients for the magnitude of their livers, one of which is said to have weighed upwards of two pounds. With this food, exquisite as it was, did Heliogabalus regale his hounds.
– Smollett

To the Reader

THIS POEM was written out of interest in a number of things: geese, country life in Ontario, Canada as an object of conversation and Edmund Spenser's *Shepherd's Calendar.*

The *Shepherd's Calendar,* published in 1579, is a collection of dialogues between shepherds named Hobbinoll, Colin, Cuddie, Piers, Thomalin, Morrell, Thenot and so on. Since there is a dialogue for each month we are able to watch a complete English year pass before our eyes with its variety of weathers, crops and animals. Hobbinoll wishes to be Colin's friend; Colin loves Rosalind for the entire calendar without any encouragement. At the end of the poem she has gone off with someone else. Cuddie is rather saucy to an old shepherd, Thenot, who reproves him with a fable about the Oak and the Briar. Willie and Thomalin discuss Cupid who has shot Thomalin in the heel and was once captured by Willie's father in a fowler's net. Piers and Palinode argue about Protestant and Catholic shepherds – which are the better. In August Willie and Perigot put on a singing match judged by Cuddie and so on. There are plaintive love-sick eclogues caused by Colin's miserable love affair, merry careless eclogues when the shepherds dance or sing and dark bitter eclogues when the sad state of the church and the poet are reviewed.

In *A Suit of Nettles* readers will notice that there are dialogues between geese named Mopsus, Branwell, Effie, Dorcas, Raymond, Duncan, Fanny and others. Branwell is the slightly ridiculous figure of melancholy itself wrapped up in a suit of nettles he has put on in order to emphasize his sorrow at a fair goose's inattention. The reader will find fables, sestinas, singing matches, the passage of a year in the Ontario countryside – many of the things already mentioned as being in the *Shepherd's Calendar.* The Church satirized in *A Suit of Nettles* is that defined by Coleridge as comprising all the intellectual institutions of the age. These institutions sometimes nourish the educational theory and the literary criticism condemned in *July* and *August,* and the mental attitude described in *May.* Scrutumnus stands for *Scrutiny,* the famous critical quarterly edited by Dr F.R. Leavis which ceased to be published some years ago. *May* arises from an incident reported in *Life* concerning some fanatics in the populous Kentucky mountains. *July* springs from a fabulous CBC *Citizens' Forum* in which Dr Hilda Neatby trounced a progressive educational theorist. The system of education suggested by Valancy's remarks resembles that of the ancient Irish bards. In the long note 'appended' to *August,* for 'God's Universe' and 'God's Tiger' read *Finnegans Wake* and Blake's *Tyger,* both victims of evaluation. In *September,* Bishop Bourget is the Pouter Pigeon, his victim is Guibord. Creighton's history of Canada, *Dominion of the North,* gives you the facts as well as the background for 'Dante's Inferno', an attempt to compress Canadian history and geography into a single horrific scenic railway ride. Some of the things said about glaciers and their products have their source in a book by L.J. Chapman and D.F. Putnam called *The Physiography of Southern Ontario.* By the way, 'Mome Fair' is a careful imitation of the annual Fall Fair held in many small Ontario towns; the prize animals, birds and flowers as well as the carnival rides. Last of all, in Ontario there are, as I count them, forty-three counties, the forty-three fields mentioned in the second eclogue.

Invocation to the Muse of Satire

With Punch's stick (he holds it in his hand)
Beat fertility into a sterile land,
With hands of hawthorn branches in the winter,
And teeth of cold March rain that bite the soft snow,
And bristly porcupines on which the hunter sits for hair;
With skin of mildew and botfly holes poked through
In hide of long impounded, ancient cow,
With eyes whose tears have quotaed out to ice long ago,
Eyes bright as the critical light upon the white snow;
With arms of gallows wood beneath the bark
And torso made of a million hooked unhooking things,
And legs of stainless steel, knives & scythes bunched together,
And feet with harrows, and with discs for shoes –
Speak, Muse of Satire, to this broken pen
And from its blots and dribbling letter-strings
Unloose upon our farm & barnyard – medicine.

With those feet, dance upon their toes
With those legs, grasp them lovingly about the thighs
With that torso, press against their breasts
With those arms, hug them black and blue
With those eyes, look at them you love
With that cheek, rub against their cheeks
With that hair, put your head down in their laps
With those teeth, give forth playful bites
And shake their hands with hour-long explorations
Of their life and heart and mind-line,
But with that stick of which new ones spring ever
From that vine where it was barbarously cut off,
Beat them about the ears and the four senses
Until, like criminals lashed in famine time,
They bring forth something; until thy goad
Grows so warm it bursts into blossoms.

Here, lady, almost blind with seeing too much
Here is the land with spires and chimneys prickly,
Here is the east of the board and here the west,
Here may you enter and there, before you depart,
May you make the sky red with doom and axey wrath.

Has no one seen the country where your cure has nursed?
It is a land of upturned privies with occupants inside them
Crawling out through new tops like astonished moths
Bursting from their unusual, foul and dark cocoons.

January

ARGUMENT: *In this first eclogue two geese, Branwell & Mopsus, discuss the different kinds of love. Branwell is wearing a suit made out of nettles.*

With the other geese within the goosehouse
There lived, I know not how, various kinds
Of geese: some like a cat, some like a mouse,
Some like a groundhog and some like lions,
Some like two straight parallel lines,
Others more circular in character,
Some shallow and some deep as mines,
Others than chaos far more muddier,
And whether you should parcel fast or loose
Some could not be but simply described 'Goose'.

[BRANWELL MOPSUS]

You there, old Mopsus, you're no bird.
I see distinctly limbs beneath the feathers;
You've got a voice too that was never heard
Just in springtime, but in all the weathers.
Do not stand agog at these green tatters;
Crossed in love I'll wear them till my death.
Mopsus, is there purpose in the pulse one gathers
Wristful by wristful? Mopsus, spend thy breath
In talking as I hear you can of geese
And life and whether they and all and life should cease.

MOPSUS

It might! And no time's better than this month,
The two-faced time whose sun no more goes south,
And in its cold there comes a milk white moth

Of frozen breath from horse and warm cow mouth
As they run down to pond to cure their drouth;
Old Brown's crowbar breaks the ice beforehand
To give new life to their lives so uncouth,
But need not do so if you understand:
By next September we could stop all life –
Let no one break the ice, let no man take a wife.

BRANWELL

But should we smother all creation outright?

MOPSUS

Here stands a woman with attractive dugs
And here a dugless wise old anchorite;
She leads a life of grotesque scarecrow hugs,
His eyes slide over Bibles slow as slugs;
She tempts you down a well of luscious shame
That into world another funeral lugs,
Another longing for the whence it came,
More jumping in and out of needles' eyes,
More love poems, paradoxes, happy unions, lies.

From some old grim geneva-gowned bore
Proto-orthodox, the hermit lifts his eyes
And gelds you from the world with sermons frore
About the cleansing of the foul heart's sties
With fasts, with baking private humble pies,
Feeling fear, dread, repentance, god-desire,
God-terror, god-damnation till you rise
Downwards from your knees to worlds of dire
Pathless woods of rungless Jacob's ladders
Set in hollows filled with aspen-voiced adders.

But do not follow either of these devils,
Reject Elijah – swear off Jezebel,
Come to my ferny groves by calm canals

Where all is bland correct and rational;
Our friendship we'll develop cell by cell,
Investigating what one can't believe;
Attached to all that is unphysical
We'll talk and muse until we must take leave.
Some call that death, but our minds meshed together
Will note the new unbodied time as but a change in weather.

Here look at man. I'll draw him in this dung.
Here the arms like shrivelled legs that uphoist
Spoons of outside world for wet mouth-tongue.
Beneath here hear his bellows groan and hiss:
Dreary East Wind sucked in bladder moist,
Expelled in warm coughs, shrieks, words, cries, alarums:
This knot hides stomach's greedy frog-jump cess,
These legs look like great dropsy ogre arms,
Here Love has chosen Sewer for his mate,
You'd marry this, you'd copy this, you'd propagate!

Climb up with me into this pea straw loft
Where rustlings strange this afternoon have come.
Above the geese Ann and the hired boy coughed,
Their bodies adding up the lovers' sum.
What oneness is there now to this relation?
Their joined mouths comprise a sort of union,
His teeth against her teeth with skull tension.
So with a short leap now his passions come.
Look how she breathes him in and out thro' snout
Of Hell, and so were we from Heaven tumbled out!

I do not think he loves her nor she him;
They love the deed, but not I think each other.
You say you love through girl her elohim,
You love her soul and not your selfish pleasure,
But how be sure? With me your steadfast brother
Be certain of the soul's affection; never
Could we stoop to this foul mad disorder.
Come Light, Fire and Sun from planets sever,

Possess the Love and Light that does not use
This stake and heart-of-vampire sexual eye of ooze.

BRANWELL

But is this light, my dear friend Mopso,
That never falls on darkness but between
The nine sick planets would to nothing go?
Can I desire one whit of world I've seen
Displayed in your cartography of spleen?
I shiver at its top, that round cold sea.
Without some isle a sea's a dismal scene.
The world's hot middle where it's he and she
Has grown for me feverish stinging clothes.
Your favourite land is better I agree –
What a round concrete continent of snows!
But too round and too continent for me
For I want offspring summerson autumnman wintersage
And tricklerain thawwind panetap upleaf windrage
Plow and seed and hoe, green, sucklepig, yellowripe,
sicklestraw and all such glamourie.

February

ARGUMENT: *Branwell's fiancée, Dorcas, has returned from a stay at the farmhouse: it turns out that she has double-crossed Branwell again and there is a big fight among the geese in the goosehouse.*

The sun begets, the moon bears, tides away
Rush into coastal caves: 'Men do bear not'
(*The Courtier*) 'their children for a day',
But women longer, for a nine moon trot;
The young cub forms like a dim loose star-knot
In the lioness as down the sun sets,
Night wobbles in, and spirit goslings sought
To dance this month through the small small eyelets
Of birth before birth, death before death pinned
Resolved & tight in each large goose egg's centre inned.

'Occurocceroo,' crowed Thompson the cock,
His small throat tied fast to the giant sun
Kicking aside the night as it rose: 'Bock!
Giddibock giddibock!' cried then each one
Of those who gave Dorcas Goose a welcome.
A pretty girl was Dorcas, a pet goose;
Back in the gooseshed was she after some
Time with a broken leg up at the house;
In the best corner sat she with her glass
Primping & being admired by all geese *en masse*.

[EFFIE DORCAS BRANWELL MOPSUS]

Where did you get that button & string
You wear so prettily around your neck?

My mistress gave me this pretty dear thing,
She loved me much, so did me pretty deck.
She gave me also corn & pease to peck,
And I learnt all the secrets of their place
When by my basket underneath Quebec[1]
The cat & dog talked all my mind could trace:
Cellar, pantry, woodshed, upstairs, downstairs!
O strange words that beat a goose's wildest nightmares!

Now these new things of which you've never heard
Let me explain; first the cellar where they
Keep preserves and roots and cream and white curd.
Butter and cheese, pitchers of milk and whey.
Close to each other, but not too, they lay
Apples, red brown and yellow in their bins,
And all in shadows deep dark down from day
Rows of cider barrels huge as dead kings,
Beside a cistern where a trapped cloud lies
Beside the air where Scug the bat scallops and flies.

He hangs from beam in winter upside down
But in the spring he right side up lets go
And flutters here and there zigzagly flown
Till up the chimney of the house quick-slow
He pendulum-spirals out in light low
Of sunset swinging out above the lawns
Gathering sinking insects' sag downflow
Returning as the light on green world dawns
And down the chimney disappears nimble
To the cellar where they catch mice with a thimble.

Catch them with cheese in thimble poised 'neath bowl.

---

1. Dorcas means a Quebec stove; unless she means
she was in Ontario which is under Quebec on a map.

This lizard-haunt bears other rooms above
Where stoves are warm when outside cold winds howl –
The pantry, dining room, the parlour clove
Apart with hallway and the kitchen move
Around me thinking of that dear gold time.
How oft, my mistress softer than a dove
Their piano bade me to play and climb
To watch the eight-day clock from their table;
Better far than sun to keep time it is able.

Old wallpapers beneath the wallpaper
Buried throughout the years in all the rooms
Over plaster, over logs their father,
Grandfather knocked clear out of wilderdom's
Green thick-boled gnarled Indian-speckled glooms.
It's a guilty house, my girls; tho' we kill
Grass blades, they killed demon scores of green elms.
A dead savage lies beneath the door-sill,
The first son[1] played cards, went to proper-church;
The second son[2] did plot beneath a beer vat much.

There are some scratches still left on the floors
Where brothers fought, where distant relatives
Once stormed the place and roasted all the doors,
But since deaths of once-possessing natives
There's been no grand excitement save when lives
Of all the males were risked in thresh-machine:[3]
Some came out alive, others half so; knives
And winnowers had quite threshed dead the others clean.
They chop down trees to build a gallows with;
Machines they build to thresh their gathered sons to death.

But the people living here are yet much
Like us: brick upon brick – they are new born,
They grow up, earn a living, learn prudence,

---

1. Family Compact. 2. Mackenzie. 3. 1914.

Depress a bed, beget a blockhead; mourn –
For the next brick seals them down, down, down, down.
And so this farmhouse stands upon the heels
Of forty-three large fields, their knot and crown.
Within, an ancient voice the silence steals:
Their heart beat, skull-hum, when it cries, are scarcely heard:
'Take us back to our beginning, white sail shipbird,

Uncut this forest old and our old countries green.'
Well girls, I now am ready for my beaus.
Pray step forward, gentlemen, and be seen.
Why by his weedy suit and burry hose
Here comes a suitor that one really knows.
Branwell it was come to welcome her back,
Long tortured with her melting shifty vows
His longing pushed him forth like a thumb tack;
He saw four buttons where was only one
So dizzed, so hoped he with a song to have her won.

BRANWELL

My love I give to you a threefold thing,
A jewsharp serenade, a song I've made
And a sparkling pretty rose diamond ring.
To haste your love to me by fate delayed.
Zing zing zing zing, azeezing, azeezing,
Azuggazing, azeezug-zug-azing.

Six reasons are there for my loving you:
Your eyes, voice, beak, legs, mind and feathers white;
Feathers like snow, like cloud, like milk, like salt,
White white against the green grass in the spring.
Oh white angel in bethlehems of grime
Teach my slow wits to understand your worth.

With only reckless hope, not the true worth
That should raise up a suitor wooing you,
I try to know that stainless mind, so white

That crystal shafts and lily mines of salt
Seem when compared coal black: and in love's spring
I beg forgiveness for my own mind's grime.

Your paddling legs do even cleanse that grime;
When I scan all your parts and all your worth,
Sometimes they seem the prettiest part of you,
Those orange sticks beneath your body white,
Those sturdy swimming oars that somersault
Above your body at the pond in spring.

When your swift beak dives down for frog offspring,
Oh resting in his bathos hut of muddy grime
How sweet to be a frog that's nothing worth
Lifted to the sublime up up by you
By your fox orange beak and neck so white,
Your beak so bright it hurts the eye like salt.

Venison needs a humble pinch of salt;
You need the sounds that from your beak do spring,
Bragful when your feet feel spring's first thaw-grime,
Stout and most vigorous and strong when worth
We argue among us; rasping when you
See robbers in the yard with moonlight white.

But most I love – that's neither orange nor white –
Your circular blue eyes intense as salt:
They shot and caught my blizzardheart for spring,
First sky they cracked into my egg of grime,
First rain they let from out your storms of worth.
For these six things then I praise and love you
And now I beg you, my dread goddess white,
To slake my dry salt lips with mercy's spring
And touch my cold grime with your golden worth.

DORCAS

Well, thank you very much but I am wed!

Here, take your ring. Before I broke my leg
In secrecy I married George.
                                        She laid,
As all intook their breaths, a large white egg.
It's George's child: the father shambles forth
A chop-the-harp and fish-with-the-strings sort of oaf.

Branwell groaned. 'My ring!' cried his friend Mopsus
'How could you give my gift to you to her,
This gynerasty ruins its victims thus!
Take that now you faithless thwarted changer!'
Down to that dungy strawy chamber's floor
Poor Branwell fell and got some kicks from George.
Dorcas waddled up upon his form there
And did the moral of it sweetly forge:

DORCAS

Beneath me girls you see a dying swan;
Beside me view a goose: which race would you breed on?

How dare you stand on top of my poor friend,
Roared Mopsus charging from his corner sulk.
He throttled Dorcas by her white wesand,
He drove his beak full deep in George's bulk;
George's stout friends then up did swiftly bulk:
Now they were Zeke Gaspar Chauncey and Dob
Hank and Hannibal, Grover and Quincy –
A big muscular stout hot gander mob
Ill temper flashing in their eyes like quinsy.
Their wings flailed down on those of Mopsus' troop
Whose agile beaks enemy flesh and feather scoop.

Nursing Dorcas as well as looking on,
Her female friends now added to the noise.
Their names were Trixy, Tilda, Jumping Joan,
Letty, Etta, Moll, Pecunia, Eloise,
Emma, Sadie as well as the two Zoes,
One black handed, the other white handed.
Their shrieks went up like rockets by small boys
Sent up when school is burnt or disbanded.
They bandaged George's wounded head and toe
But Mopsus' broken men they pummelled to and fro.

Past the mash trough, bran tub and water pan
Mopsus' allies were pressed sore hard at first;
But soon past pan, past tub, past trough George ran
Chased by Raymond a goose for blood athirst,
A goose who longed to see George in a hearse.
Three times he chased poor George round the mash trough,
Shouting vengeance on those who hated verse.
Just then to see what eggs she might take off
Ann came with pail; her boots were stuck with snow.
All battle ends as all to taste this latter go.

March

ARGUMENT: *Branwell and Effie compare world pictures; his is understandably rather gloomy. For good measure Effie recites a fable about the doorknob and the door which argues for having some sort of handle to your life whether you believe in it or not. Mopsus condescends to Effie as if she were too bluestocking for him; actually from his speeches later on you will see that Effie's attitude has had a great influence upon him.*

[BRANWELL EFFIE MOPSUS]

Lord, Lord, Effie, what fills you with such joy?
You are the drudge and scullion of this place
And yet you're lively as a wind-up toy.
You reach beneath each sitting goose with grace
And turn their eggs with pleasure on your face.
I'd puke at my hand being warmed that way;
I wince at how we reproduce our race.
How can you stand to do this night and day?
To midwife scores of cherubs into Hell
When you have reason to and can its horrors tell.

Did not your mother curse you as she died
After you'd changed her dressings for ten years;
Did she not often call you to her side
To twist your wing or box you on your ears?
Did she not fill all suitors' hearts with fears
That your womb could not nourish any seed?
She was to you what Dorcas was to me;
Love dreams, Love fails; Hate wakes and Hate succeeds,
For this is what rules fire earth air and sea –
A trapper with a trap of natural laws
That closes on all animals its starry jaws.

EFFIE

When we were small, Branwell, you thought not so.
We both then seemed to know of somewhere else
Than water earth and air and fire although
These things now seem all that is universe.
I dreamt I saw a white walled garden once
Where a child sat playing on a panpipe
Made, it seemed, of twinkling golden straw.
He stopped and asked me how I liked its shape;
I said its like for grace I never saw;
He said its straws were cut from a farm
In which our universe of stars is but a stone

Sulking in fields of dew it cannot see.
Branwell, I took my heart and opened it
To better hear his strange glad minstrelsy.
The shortest straw did to that dark place flit;
Its everlasting music makes me fit
To live through all ingratitude and dread,
Rage, boredom and soul-starving deficit.
If I prevent these eggs from being addled
You must not sneer; this egg may hatch a heart
That will not close itself against a golden dart.

BRANWELL

Well, I've a dream that strongly counters yours,
I dream I am surrounded by the moons,
All twenty-eight silvery pock-faced whores:
The New and Old Moons, the in-between ones,
The Full Moon broad and fat and weighing tons,
The Dark Moon, the Black Moon which no one sees,
A mummy of dried tar that love's mind shuns.
Their circle spins about me silver, green and gold.
I rush at what seems young and always grasp what's old,
More new than new, more old than old, the Black Moon cold,
A faggot-limbed, burlap-papped scarecrow stuffed with mould.

My days, if they are days, are different too:
I think we get our pleasure from grasping
Difference and likeness; these I now eschew.
I used to see a rat and then observe a robin,
But now the bird seems but a rat with wings;
A rose is but a rat without its legs, turned –
Turned inside out to get the whites and pinks,
A sunset's but a wide rat thoroughly burned,
We geese are large rats stuck all over with feathers
A rat's breath cold & dry & hot & moist explains
the winds and weathers,
So nothing has difference, therefore nothing is the same;
All things twin, all things opposed vanish in my doubt's
marsh-flame.
Sometimes a nest of angels in the sun steal in my eyes like thieves.
I banish them by rolling on the ground in this suit
of nettle-leaves.

EFFIE

Branwell, our dreams are quite alike you know.
My white wall is the moons that round you go.
My garden is your glade where eight and score
Torment a dying world that's lost its lore
Of weaving into charms that shine a star,
Nail whirlwinds and make spades of swords of war,
Raise up the dead – the simple speakable air;
And of my piping child you are the fallen heir.
Branwell, I'll tell to you a curious tale
I once saw scratched upon a rusty pail
Thrown where the dungheaps in the barnyards start.
I spent the summer getting this by heart
And you too, Mopsus, listen if you must;
Women may also entertain the mind, I trust.
THERE was a Doorknob and a Door,
The former white and rather poor,
Yet handy for those going through
From hall to kitchen fro and to.

The door was made of solid pine,
Dark brown and varnished slick and fine;
'Doorknob!' said Door, 'you pale weak thing,
You spoil the look of me your king.
You dumb-bell clinging to my grandeur,
Asymmetry I can't endure.'

'Door, Door,' said Knob, 'What you are now
Is yet beyond my puzzling brow.
Your voice is like the sound of snow
Heard in mind of summer rainbow,
Or dumb seedless lumps of dark zinc
When green leaves try to on them think.
But though I cannot you define
I still know the successful line
To keep door, door – doorknob, doorknob:
To think by day is half my job,
To size up each approaching hand
And fit it with a surface bland;
I turn as smoothly as I can
To hand of wife and child and man;
When day is over then neap tide
Of dreams drowns all my day's neat pride;
Whales of Lust and Rays of Hate,
Madness like Eel and Fear like Skate
Swim rough and tumble in my mind;
Devouring all sane things they find
They warn me what net I must choose,
What hook & trident, leaden shoes,
Harpoons or cages I must use
When I do wake the following day
Beside the day-sea's voyage way
That leads through clouds of thoughts & hands
Unto again these dreamy sands
Where how to progress, how retreat
I learn for climbing world-life's street.'

'Leave off! Shut up!' shouted the Door,

'I'll not believe you any more.
You shouldn't have been to me tacked;
When I've lost you what have I lacked?
There! There!' The Door convulsed and shook.
Knob snapped in two and Door forsook;
Rattling across two floors it rolled.
'Robbers!' the farmer's wife carolled,
Awakening at the snapping sound.
Fierce as famished ravenous bloodhound
Farmer Smith sailed down the front stairs,
Night shirt flying, old hands flexed
To rid his house with robbers vexed.
Above the kitchen now his boys,
All five waked also with the noise.
Down like hail they came to kitchen
Tripping pails their ma kept swill in.
What thunder from the hallway where
Old Smith's loud crash does quake the air.
He misses knob and hits closed door.
His sons cry 'In the hall is robber!'
Crashing through door themselves they went
Through to hall and punch old gent,
Who bellows out with counter whack,
Pushing his five sons back, back, back.
Thus back and forth until the Door,
Crazed into splinters, was no more.
It lighted lamps for many a year,
Its knob was toy to children dear,
Still thinking, dreaming, showing them
How to be Ham, Japhet and Shem
And drunken Noah as all men must
Who for the height of being lust.

MOPSUS

Ham, Shem, Drunken Noah? What does it mean?

BRANWELL

The meaning's felt often before it's seen;
My heart knows what my rusted mind does not.
Thank you, Effie. Such moments have I sought
When I might smile or pick at such a knot
As logic fingers could not ravel out at once.

MOPSUS

I shall not sleep a wink thinking of this.
A sibyl come to out of her cave she is.
Perhaps we'll take you along to Mome Fair
To explain the merry-go-round there,
The Ferris wheel & the sideshows to us.

EFFIE

But I always go to the fair, Mopsus,
And not one of these eggs but will be there too
Next September – for a general *nostalgie de la boue.*

April

ARGUMENT: *With Duncan as judge the geese hold a bardic contest in honour of Spring.*

[DUNCAN RAYMOND VALANCY]

Here is a kernel of the hardest winter wheat
Found in the yard delicious for to eat.
It I will give to that most poetic gander
Who this season sings as well as swam Leander.
The white geese with their orange feet on the green
Grass that grew round the pond's glassy sheen
Chose then Valancy and Raymond to sing
And to hear them gathered about in a ring.

RAYMOND

I speak I speak of the arable earth,
Black sow goddess huge with birth;
Cry cry killdeers in her fields.

Black ogress ate her glacier lover
When the sun killed him for her;
The white owl to the dark crow yields.

Caw caw whir whir bark bark
We're fresh out of Noah's Ark;
Wild geese come in arrowheads

Shot from birds dead long ago
Buried in your negro snow;
Long water down the river sleds.

Black begum of a thousand dugs,

A nation at each fountain tugs;
The forests plug their gaps with leaves.

Whet whet scrape and sharpen
Hoes and rakes and plows of iron;
The farmer sows his sheaves.

Mr Sword or Mr Plow
Can settle in your haymow,
All is the same to Mother Ground.

Great goddess I from you have come,
Killdeer crow geese ditch leaf plowman
From you have come, to you return
In endless laughing weeping round.

VALANCY

Your limbs are the rivers of Eden.
From the dead we see you return and arise,
Fair girl, lost daughter:
The swallows stream through the skies,
Down dipping water,
Skimming ground, and from chimney's foul dusk
Their cousins the swifts tumble up as the tusk
Of roar day
In bright May
Scatters them gliding from darkness to sun-cusp.

Your face unlocks the bear from his den.
The world has come into the arms of the sun.
What now sulky earth?
All winter you lay with your face like a nun,
But now bring forth
From river up boxdrain underground
Fish crawling up that dark street without sound
To spawn
In our pond

Young suckers and sunfish within its deep round.

Your body is a bethlehem.
Come near the sun that ripened you from earth
Pushing south winds
Through lands without belief till this pretty birth
The faithful finds:
Fanatic doves, believing wrens and orioles
Devoted redwinged blackbirds with their calls,
Archilochus alexandri,
Melospiza georgiana,
All surround you with arched cries of Love's triumphals.

Your mind is a nest of all young things, all children,
Come to this meadow forest edge;
Put her together
From this squirrel corn dogtooth young sedge
And all this weather
Of the white bloodroots to be her skin
The wake robin to be her shin
Her thighs pockets
Of white violets
Her breasts the gleaming soft pearly everlasting.

For her limbs are the rivers of Eden;
Her face unlocks
The brown merry bear from his den,
From his box
The butterfly and her body is a bethlehem
Humming
With cherubim
And her mind is a cloud of all young things, all children.

The prize to this one goes cried eagerly some
And others cried that to Raymond it must come,
So that Duncan Goose turned to the plantain leaf
And chopped the prize in half with beak-thrust brief.

May

ARGUMENT: *Effie and Fanny are discovered drynursing the entire flock of goslings. Fanny describes how two propagandists recently roaming the backwoods have met an interesting fate.*

[EFFIE FANNY]

I think that yours will turn out white
And mine will be the gray ones
But all just now are furry bright
Like infant furry pocket suns.

Goslings now, goslings all
Run not near the muskrat's hall
Dancing weasel might prance up.

Yours will be white, mine will be gray,
Some day now in the future,
But neither goose nor gander they
Now play in tender nurture.

Goslings there, goslings dear
Swim not to those rushes near
Waiting skunk might on you sup.

Pray what's the news of snapping turtles
And what of snapping foxes
We fend, we guard, we watch for rascals
That snatch our goslings from us.

FANNY

To be worse for I heard from a cousin
Who was down here loading caddises & cressing

That two strange geese of the scientific variety
Had preached all year for their society,
You do know how big the families are back there,
Forty-two or fifty-two goslings is not a thing rare.
The section is so overpopulated,
It puffs up and over with children inflated,
These two ladies want to save all the hill country women
From all that labour and child-labouring.
'I've got the greatest news for you,' they juicy say,
To some farm wife who looks like a big five ring circus tent
Held down by small children holding on it.
'We can show you how to stop this torment to-day,
We can show you how to stop conceiving & bearing children.'
They open up their big black boxes then:
'This piece of straw, this frazzled bit of string, this old
Button from a castrati's overcoat at his death sold,
Worth twenty babes any day and all free!'
Well, some places they caused a riot jamboree,
And some other places the people didn't catch on what
They meant. 'To bring forth children never not –
Who now could want that desert barren state?' they said.
'But you could have one or plan for two, plump & decent fed
And warmly clothed,' these smooth ladies rejoined.
'You then could buy yourself a kill-yourself-if-you-touch-it
And a watch-everybody-squeeze-up-from-hell-while-you-sit;
An electric jelly-fish warmer than a husband to go to bed with you
And a pass-like-a-vulture-shadow and get your sons to do
Two-backed tricks in the back and flatten 5,000,000 frogs too.'
'But,' said the people, 'we like having more, once joined;
And one doesn't raise as well as a dozen and a half.
You grow us more food and wages, smarty;
Meanwhile we'll keep hoeing our own kindergarty.
Just how could one huge cow rest its heart on one little calf?
Children are our life, our bread and our clothing,
With their two little arms & legs & their one head
They come toppling shouting out of us to prove we're not dead.
Can God not damn you for hating being?'
Now then the two biddies came to the conclusion

After a year of very little success that pretty soon
They'd have to go back when one night they met
Coming up a hill toward them two handsome yet
Sort of grim rakish sly curly young men who looked just like.
'Why you slick ladies aren't going farther
In this wet and no-dry-hotel-for-miles weather?'
'We can suffer far more than this for the cause of no-tyke.
The more it rains on us, the more we laugh,
It can't wet us with what we waxy know; we scoff
At rain and suffer to decrease humanity: we're glad
To outwit any fertility.' The two brothers bade
Them come for food & shelter to their house.
They went, more than slightly attracted, to this place.
It was old, mossy roofed & gabled with many windows
Set between leafy thick appletree rows.
The brothers asked these expert girls to be their wives.
First these spinsters said not by the beard of their chinny lives.
At length to a ceaseless mad tattooing
Of caresses they allowed the brothers' wooing
And made their special preparations for the bridal night.
They tied the brothers up in sheets of tight
Glass, beaten gold, cork, rubber, netting, stoppers, sand;
They themselves dammed their wombs with a pretty skillful hand
And lay back waiting for the sensation
Of an interesting lively copulation,
Without any of the disfiguring after effects necessary for population.
Nevertheless and oh nevertheless
The brothers so handled their part of the process
That in six weeks' time the ladies in question were with child,
Seeded down by those strange men dark & wild.
'How on earth did you do this to us, Roderick?'
They groaned & shrieked & roared. 'And you too, dreadful Benedict!'
'Madams, we are twins,' the brothers explained,
'And for centuries our old family has gained
New members for itself always in twos or threes or fours.
Our emblem is a white sow with twelve pigs
All sucking her dry, like bishops in periwigs
All translating at a Holy Bible, and *you* we picked

To test our fertile power on since you kicked
Our family's sense of lively birth in the teeth.
From this day may you billow saw waddle gag groan beneath
The ripeness of a Nile in bringing forth!'
A dark cloud swept thunderously down from the North
Of snapping turtles, newts & hopping toads; as in a dream
The women's loins poured forth a swollen stream
Until the brothers moved them to their granary
Where they were turned into strong & sturdy machinery;
One into a large & squat fanning mill,
The other to a tall conical cylindrical
Iron Maiden used for threshing seeds from ripe sunflowers.
So usefully did end the lives of those insistent life devourers.

June

ARGUMENT: *Branwell is still suffering from Dorcas' defection. A huge gray owl seems always to be taunting him.*

[MOPSUS BRANWELL]

Now is the ox-eyed daisy out
  Out now everywhere,
The bobolink tips his wings
In the humming blue gold air.

The wild rose opens simple eyes
  In a green briar face,
The mourning dove beats a drum
In a drowsy shady place.

The strawberry like a wren's heart
Shows beneath three green leaves,
The garter snake leaves behind
One of his silver glittering crystal annual sleeves.

Branwell, where have you wandered now
That seem as sad as snow on bough
And can't look like the time.
What can be better than this weather –
The wind made out of red clover
The clouds as white as rime.

BRANWELL

I have been shooting with my gun
At a bird that eats my sun;
It seems a hooting owl
Large, moping, gravid, dismal, gray.

I saw it flit beneath a dray
That large sad dreary fowl
But when I shot it out of this
It flew unharmed up with a hiss
Onto a shadowy beam.
And when I shot again it flew
Out to blight the fields' green hue
Into the gray of dream.
Whereafter this ash bird threw back
My leaden bullets of attack
Solemnly laughing then.
My friend, I now give up the fight
Endless as that of day and night
And stand accursed among men.

MOPSUS

My father knew of such a bird,
It made all life seem edgeless, blurred
And sat upon his head
Fouling his shoulders and his hair,
Raising its young in that strange lair
And vomiting up the dead.
He never stirred to shoo it off
But waited late and long enough
Until it sank from sight.
Soft answered did its wrath dissolve
And sink into the gay revolve
Of his thoughts so light.
He looks a little like an owl
But still is human, toe to jowl,
And merrier than ever.
To fight that bird were downright folly
For her name is Melancholy.

BRANWELL

No, I cannot patient your advice,
I can only twist in the hard vise
Of her betrayal.
She took my presents all to him,
She gave him all her treasure slim
While talking our betrothal.
This found I lately in a lost
Letter in the orchard grass.
The small bur basket that I stuck together for her
She left out in the rain until unstuck.
When she would hardly let me take her arm
She gave her beak entire to that gross buck.

  I am like a hollow tree
Where the owl & weasel hide
  I am like a hollow tree

Dead in the forest of his brothers.

My feet are sensitive as brains
Put hats upon them
My feet are sensitive as brains
All the ground is grassed with knives.

These fingers that once played
Nimbly the harp
These fingers that once played
Are soft & suck as leeches.

My throat where once a song
Flew out like a golden bird
My throat where once a song
Is a woodpecker's bitten door.

My eyes are the entrances
To the kingfishers' nests
My eyes are the entrances
Tunnels of clay lined with fish bones.

I see the red sun sink
For the last time this far north.
The full moon rises: my thoughts fly forth.
Leap forth, oh bird of prey & turncoat ermine,
Nebula out of my mind
That swampy fair
Where the bittern pumps from its cistern of despair.

July

ARGUMENT: *Valancy & Anser compare methods of educating the young goslings. Anser is their schoolmaster.*

[ANSER VALANCY]

Hohum there, Valancy. What brings you down to the gosling school?

VALANCY

Well, I went to the granite boulder in the pasture and I found you weren't there. When I was a gosling, Old Strictus sometimes held the school in the hollow where there used to be a cabin but you weren't there either. Why have you moved the school to this boggy acre?

ANSER

The goslings voted that we move it here. The crickets are very plentiful hereabouts and so are the young frogs and lizards.

VALANCY

Indeed you are different from my old teacher. He alone had the vote in our school and if we didn't come to school he searched us out from the grass in which we were hiding with a strong thrumming dig of his old yellow beak.

ANSER

You cannot educate the young goslings by fear. Nor by breaking their will; you must persuade them to prefer herdsgrass to bladder campion. You should not beak the child.

VALANCY

I like what you say. Where are your students by the way?

ANSER

It's the boy's fault. He's told to watch us you know, but look at him. He has fallen asleep as indeed I did myself. When he's asleep my students steal into the fields of pease and buckwheat and gorge themselves to their heart's content. Don't frown at that. They are happy. Let them be happy.

VALANCY

Well Anser, I agree that you should persuade rather than force them. But I don't think that applies to their attendance. I mean surely they must be here, or how can you persuade them?

ANSER

You are rather conventional in your views and I think you will soon realize that you are attacking a good thing. You'll soon see, I think, that the rule does indeed apply even to their attendance. You see the subject I teach them is taught to them even when they are not here – not physically present.

VALANCY

Good Lord! What do you teach them?

ANSER

Now first, my friend, whatever did that pedagogue of such renown, Old Strictus, teach you as a gosling?

VALANCY

When I was a gosling he taught us to know the most wonderful list of things. You could play games with it; whenever you were bored or miserable what he had taught you was like a marvellous deck of cards in your head that you could shuffle through and turn over into various combinations with endless delight. At the end of the year we each made ourselves little huts of burdock leaves, lay down on our backs with large stones on our bellies and recited the whole thing over to ourselves forwards and backwards. Some of the poorer students were in those huts till November but even those to whom it was an agony, when they at length did know that they knew all that a young goose was supposed to know, the moment when they rolled the stone away and climbed out of their burdock hut – it was as joyous a moment as if they had been reborn into another world.

ANSER

Well, well, well. Might I ask just what this reviving curriculum was?

VALANCY

Who are the children of the glacier and the earth?
Esker and hogsback, drumlin and kame.
What are the four elements and the seven colours,
The ten forms of fire and the twelve tribes of Israel?
The eight winds and the hundred kinds of clouds,
All of Jesse's stem and the various ranks of angels?
The Nine Worthies and the Labours of Hercules,
The sisters of Emily Brontë, the names of Milton's wives?
The Kings of England and Scotland with their Queens,
The names of all those hanged on the trees of law
Since this province first cut up trees into gallows.
What are the stones that support New Jerusalem's wall?
Jasper and sapphire, chalcedony, emerald,
Sard, sardius, chrysolite, beryl, topaz,
Chrysoprasus, hyacinthine and amethyst.

ANSER

My goodness, how useless so far as the actual living of life is concerned. Why we have simplicity itself compared to what that maze of obscurity was. I mean since our heads are going to be chopped off anyhow we only teach the young gosling what he likes.

VALANCY

We liked what Strictus taught though it took some effort.

ANSER

Pah! If they like nothing, then teach them that. The self must be free.

August

ARGUMENT: *Raymond chances upon a famous critic-goose's funeral. Whose ghost actually appears: apparently it has been raised after a bout of its favourite activity – putting poems into order of merit.*

[RAYMOND LOBO BLOT BUSTO
TERPSICHORE SCRUTUMNUS]

Is not this trenchant Lobo? Is not
This Busto and Mr Amos Blot?
Surely these are the Nine Muses
And these the Furies with lighted fuses
And these the Graces one taking, two giving –
All mourning one no longer living
But dead within his pale blue coffin,
A child perhaps no longer laughing.
Ah! what a crowd of mourners here
All dressed in black each with his tear.

LOBO

Go bid the soldiers shoot
Go bid each screech owl hoot
For Scrutumnus he is dead
Who contained in his wee head
A sharper sense of good and bad
Than all the ages' gooses had.

BLOT

Go bid the women shriek and cry.
Go bid them black their dresses dye.
He who first showed how to choose

Between the fast, between the loose,
The connoisseur of crickets' songs
Who knew his harps and knew his gongs
Died ere his precious work was done.
Died and veiled with tar our sun.

BUSTO

The song of gull and hawk and shrike
He first discovered, first did like.
The fancy wren, the too sweet lark
He bravely thrust down into dark.
The language of the common sparrow,
The music of the untaught farrow
Held he sweeter far than thrushes
Whistling silver trills and rushes.
Pigs and sparrows sing 'We copulate,'
And mean exactly what they state.

RAYMOND

Egad! Who was this Tamburlaine,
Who said bluebirds sing like a chilblain
And made old reputations fall
Like feathery snow from Mother Holl.

LOBO

Scrutumnus! Scrutumnus! Scrutumnus!
We lay this wreath on thy tumulus!
A wreath of thy favourite pigsweed
And lambsquarters gone to seed.
Bring on the songs and we will play
His favourite game upon this day.

BLOT

Ladies and gentlemen, after I've sung

These three songs from my leather lung
Establish a preference among the three,
But evaluate judiciously.

THE FIRST SONG

Snort we and grunt we, love,
   Pigs in the sties of Venus,
The fairest pair e'er transformed, love,
   For Circe's circus.

Swink we and sweat we, sweet,
   Guzzling our julep amorous
From the great she-wolf's teat
   A strange Remus & Romulus.

Though we puppets dally
   'Tis the theatre of a god;
Though this pintel rudely rally
   What puts it out – a lotus pod.

Clapclapclapclapclapclapclapclap

THE SECOND SONG

Like to a dewdrop was thy love to me
That glitters sweetly in the morn's new light,
Fairer than any in that jewelled sea
Fastened upon the bank's high bosky height.

Alas, when I had climbed your face to sight
Through all the prickets' grasping stings & snags,
I found that you had long since taken flight
Enamoured of my rival's golden bags.

Clapclapclapclap

Rubicund cherub, thy wings waft
Stars planets clouds kingdoms past;
My cordial soul its humid clout
Ignite and set ablaze.

Blue vivid seraph with thy wand
Glittering with golden words inscribed
Promiscuous and tangled
   Mnemonically wave.

Candid Spirit, pure as the Sun of Sun
Come, oh come O Angel with a pen,
Inhabit this prepared twelve-tribed den
Thy cradled, crossed and rising
   Song to bring forth.
Hmh.
Now quickly without conferences
Hand in the noted preferences.
Erato here prefers the first, I see,
And you the second, fond Melpomene;
Why Urania, you have liked the third!
Shortly before his death Scrutumnus heard
And judged these songs; the first!
By John Dong he adjudged the first!
The second by Edmund Lily Goose
Comes second! he said he found it loose
With no real emotion urging it on,
The images overdecorous and overdrawn.
The third he found obscure, a farrago
Of bad English and worse Latin lingo,
No real emotion, no language of the people,
Immoral in its basic avoidance of simplicity,
Pompous overblown fantastically …

TERPSICHORE

But you and Scrutumnus, sir, do not
Understand these songs. One ought
To see that each has a different purpose
And therefore a different word choice,
You do not laugh at a cat or a frog
Because they cannot act like a hog.

BLOT

I do, madam. You are wrong, wench!

LOBO

Who's this skirted lesbian stench?

BUSTO

Take her prisoner! Tie her down.
We'll give her a green gown.
Give me my pruning hook & sword cane.
Now where my shadow falls on this bane
I'll spare, but where it does not fall
I'll cut an offering for his funeral.

RAYMOND

Your shadow is much shorter than her form.

LOBO

Then she must bow to him, for he's the norm.

RAYMOND

Which will he cut? Her head or her feet?

BUSTO

I'll cut her head. Here Nymph so fleet,
In dancing your abominations
Dance no more on the honest man's sensations.
Nymph of Sciolism, my honest shears convect,
My desire is constative with my effect!

RAYMOND

Fortunately no one can kill a Muse
Unless their own to kill they choose.
To kill his own genius is all he can do.
What is this unmelodious hullabaloo
And smell of sulphur? Scrutumnus, Thou!

THE SHADE OF SCRUTUMNUS[1]

Aooh! Bow wowwowwowwowwowwow

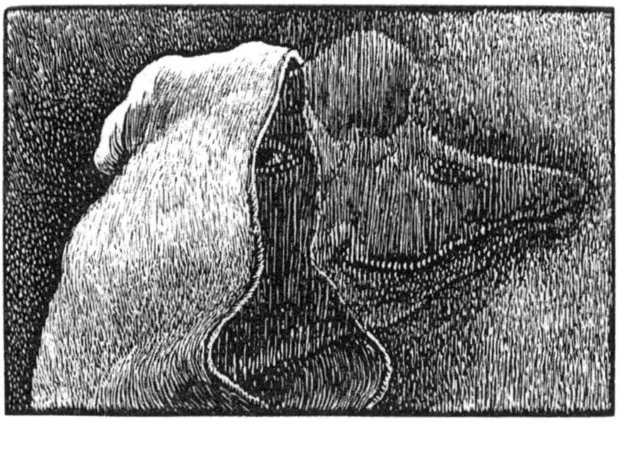

RAYMOND

Why little man what is this harp you have here
With a spider in it?

THE SHADE

Mine! Mine, do you hear?
And no one shall take it from me!

---

1. The critical judgements of Scrutumnus are deservedly famous. Once on being shown a great marble palace of exquisite beauty, he exclaimed, 'That little outhouse across the way has more real sincerity.' When first told the story of the little princes in the Tower he exclaimed how much they must have got on Richard III's nerves and how dark passionate energies were to be preferred to stagnant frozen purities. Often his friends' mouths fell open at the audacity and the courage his determination to speak out entailed. When a person in the goosehouse was showing forth the wonders of the universe – the stars, the Milky Way, mountains, etc., he complained that the Universe was needlessly obscure and he rather wondered if God had simply not played an elaborate joke on us all. 'I think God gathered a little coterie around him of admiring sycophantic angels who praised whatever he did,' said Scrutumnus, 'no matter how hideously entangled.' But his most famous critical *mot* was his judgement of God's Tiger: looking at it very, very closely and making some sensitive observations on the beauty of the stripe work he said – turning to the hind legs – that it was too bad after such a splendid beginning that God had scamped the conclusion of this noble creation. Someone asked him what he meant by this; he said, 'Why can't you see? The hind legs are almost identical with the front legs. He has merely repeated the first idea for the front legs, and has not been able to work out a proper conclusion to his work at all.'

September

ARGUMENT: *In the farmhouse world Peter & Ann get married just in time: in the goose world you see Mome Fair as our geese see it. There are exhibits of prize animals & plants, the rides, a remarkable funhouse, sideshows and a preacher who is roaring drunk. George & Dorcas particularly liked the Ferris wheel, Mopsus the merry-go-round, Effie the sideshows and Bramwell went into the funhouse again & again for another look at the horse-eating iris.*

By parents strong pegged young Peter and Ann
Were wedded in welter by waspish minister.
Home had they hugged huge bride with child
When wonder! wonder! wawled soon infant;
Ceremony, wed-supper, then son and heir.
Haw haw such haste, hiccoughed the gathering ...

MOME FAIR

THE BLIND FIDDLER plays just inside the gate

THE POUTER PIGEON
proudly pouts at window,
Crozier and cap and scarlet carillon.
Heretic helmet dove's hearse rolls up,
'Stone it shakers! Stone it my doves!'
Peevishly primps out Pouter Pigeon stiff,
But barbs brotherly bury poor heretic,
Coat with concrete his coffin fearing that
Pouter Pigeon may perhaps pry him up.
Beautiful boomchested Bishop Pouter
Commands croppers to carve out other graves,
Fetch the faithful finikins to new place,
Sell this site to slaked-lime makers,

Confident of course that the concrete's tough.

THE CAT

Gracious gracious gallant galvanizing puss
Sleek satin hide and secretion eyes:
In the morn innocent indecent exposure,
PM perambulates puckishly pussies in restaurants,
Corrosive urine crackles in crazed urinal,
Dim bannisters dally his dumpling dairy maid,
Yowls he in Yonge Street of yare conquest ...
Postcoit pining pans him to early bed,
But TWO finds him tootling untiringly meeow flute.

THE DOG

Feisty fugleman, frowsy small dog
Yipped and yapped and yowled and growled,
Teasing travellers on track of blessing quest,
Lifted a leg at lustrous silk parasols,
Slept when the silky sage thief came tripping,
Disgusted the dewy white damsel Moon.

THE PIG

Pink protrusion, pachyderm pork crystal,
Crackling with conch sounds casual acorn;
Mice muzzle and masticate your back
Unbeknownst by unquick ununquiet mind;
Hear nothing ears except earhasp twitch,
Smell nothing snout except swine incense,
Touch nothing trotters save tapioca sty wallow:
Eyes examine the excellent nose horizon,
Heedless of huntsmen horning your oak hall,
Dreaming of the devoured peacock safe down in your belly.

THE HEN

Hohum humble hiked herself to Sunday School,
Never nudged neck up to sky,
Looked late & soon longingly downward,
Found foody scraps, fetched them to others,
Dug in the dunghill – her delight by the hour,
Pecked not the pants of the puerile kicker,
Rebuked not the ribald rooster's oppressions,
Stood the steal-weasel's sucking all eggs of hers,
Forgave the fox for chewing her wing,
Fine eggs, fair feathers, fat carcass, old hen.

THE COW

Fanciful flighty fairy cow,
Black & white bulging beautiful thing.
Burdock bites she busily out of barn door,
Slavers till sicked over salt block at gate.
New grass assaulted at stone boat by her,
Cagily corn she corrals over barbed wire,
Tree leaves tassel out twitching mouth,
New clover now navigates she through gate,
Gorges down googols of juicy green fodder,
Bloats her four bellies up balloonwise-zeppelin,
Mooing for mercy meanders to keeper-help
Who sticks her with sharp pen, soon rush out
All vapours as velvety voluptuous tongue darts
Out again.

THE CLOSED GENTIAN

Gentlefolk gentian purple gentleman flower
First prize finds fuzzy buzz seekers after gold,
Golden manners, golden heart, golden gold cellar-hidden;
Cellar-kept, for closed gentian cruelly stays shut,
Shut, shut shameless hand, shamble-soul plant:
Traps robber tumbled in tenacious for honey:

Stinking beauty, star-hell sterile-pregnant gentian.

AMPERSAND the ewe, mare, cock and drake, rose caterpillar and cheese.

DANTE'S INFERNO & FUNHOUSE

Rivière du Loup 1. A huge gasping gaping jaw narrowing to rapids.
Castor grassus 2. A small room padded with beaver fur.
Montreal 3. A room painted with demon faces, arms
Niagara Falls holding out white dogs, drums beating, rushing
roaring sound.
Louis XV 4. A shower of milk and a swarm of honeybees.[1]
5. Freezing cold passage way, lamprey eels pursued
Moraviantown by Latvians; an old Indian's skin is turned into
horse-whips and shoelaces, deafening explosion.
Mackenzie 6. A bloody divan wearing a lace fichu awaits you
in this room.
Dawson Road 7. Go fast through this steam chamber where a
Batoche Red Nose[2] glowing confronts an Eye[3] glaring. A
White Horse is also having quite a time with a
monster horse-eating iris which has NEVER
Regina FORGET printed on its petals. A pouter pigeon
struts by.
8. This room seems like a railway carriage
Craigellachie running on a monorail attached to the crotches of
a row of bearded gentlemen all standing in a row
with tophats on.
Laurier 9. You are smoking a pipe; the conductor says,
'Defense de fumer.'
1912 10. A Tiger yowls by with a lady on his back.[4]

---

1. Anointment with milk and honey was part of French coronation rites.
2. Macdonald.
3. Riel.
4. The election was fought over reciprocity with the U.S.A. A favourite opposition poster.

11. The train comes to grief in a drift of flourdough.

12. You stumble into a room where a man is being trepanned: a lineup of 100,000 are all
1914 waiting to be in deathly silence. Accompanying you is a pale beaver type: everyone has him. He is continually telling you to duck ghost cobwebs.

13. A horrible smell fills the room: every time the
1937 attendants try to turn on ventilating fans a group of stately voices say, 'No. You are interfering with the right to smell.'[5]

14. Another room lined with freshly bleeding
1942 scalps. A small spiral tunnel, rather messy, leads you to a beach where sea serpents and glass bubbles float towards you. These disappear and
Port Moody you are back at the fair again stepping over a dead warrior with flaxen hair who must have tried to get in the wrong way and going by a simply exhausted old harridan in a cage who is trying to sell tickets to it.

THE MERRY-GO-ROUND

Out of French chivalry comes an endless string of gracefully up and downing wooden horses all pursuing a brass ring labelled TRUTH and it *is* TRUTH. Loafkneaders and genitalmen, I will describe to you these jumping up and down beasts as they sail by. I; we have here a really stock
Parmenides still stoneheavy big Percheron that does not go up and down like the others because as a matter of fact he doesn't believe in it. II; a fiery steed! it

---

5. 'The Judicial Committee of the Privy Council judicially condemned virtually any national plan to cope with any Canadian depression.' Creighton, *Dominion of the North.* In short, Bennett's New Deal interfered with the right of the provinces to be depressed.

Heraclitus goes up and down like nothing but and its whole
form keeps flowy-changing; as a matter of fact
you can't seem to sit in the same saddle twice on
it it seems. III; here's a beautiful white horse –
peculiar – it's got a beeyootiful glass horse sailing
Plato above it and the horse you're sitting on keeps
looking up in the most sort of ridiculous way
trying to do exactly what the glass horse is doing
but of course it just looks like a cheap imitation
particularly since it keeps looking up all the time
and the beautiful glass horse has such poise it
never looks anywhere except straight ahead. IV; a
rather stocky Clydesdale with three saddles, three
Aristotle heads and three buttocks: one buttock is too
hairy, the middle one is just right and the left
hand one has no hair at all. V; just behind him is
Democritus a very shifty galloway – all sand as a matter of
fact, all whirling around and you're in danger of
sinking into your saddle up to your topknot. VI;
Epicurus Here's a drunken old nag with a wreath of
poppies slung about its neck. VII; a sorry nag with
its bottom up in the air because it's subduing its
Zeno bottom and that's the surest way of tiring your
bottom out. Its skin is all leathery; it leathers it
by beating it against the walls of its stall so that if
anyone *should* beat it, you see, why it wouldn't
feel this at all. VIII; Next we have a horse
St Augustine looking extremely thoughtful – no wonder his
rear quarters are half pitch dark and half blinding
white and no amount of dye will ever get the
beast either one colour or the other. There's a
certain marionette like quality about this horse's
prancing as if every capriole were destined by
some other force than the horse's mind. This
horse wears a certain self satisfied look on his face
as if he knew a secret nightmare no one else did.
Aquinas IX; a very fat round mare slops by looking as if
she bore twin foals, one maybe a classic stallion

and the other a milkwhite unicorn filly unified
within her. Well, let her amble by. X; Trotting
behind her is a lean pale horse who smirks at her
Duns Scotus girth and completeness and seems to wear always
a knowing look as if let's not talk about a full
manger laid up in heaven when work is over but
let's have a look at just a wisp of hay here right in
front of me. XI; what a pretty snow white horse
Boehme tattooed with stars, mountains meadows real
sheep moving on them it seems & fiery comets
& ships in a harbour & little horses dancing in a
barnyard. This horse's eyes – oh the angelic
aurora wonder of its gold red mane. Every once in
a while this horse's colour completely changes.
People shy away then I can tell you! Storms break
out in the tattooed skies and a fiery fire burns in
the eyes. However, it bubbles over – a light
comes into his eyes and the world changes back
again. XII; Now here comes a smart little fossil
Descartes horse large as a fox ticking as if it worked
mechanically with melted beeswax in its feedbag
and a distinctly mathematical looking hoof (it
could add I'm sure if it were let loose) as well as a
tendency to go for weighty things like lumps of
coal you may hand him: but he doesn't go for
painted butterflies or candy sugar sticks. XIII; a
Hobbes brutish nasty and short small fat merrylegs of a
pit pony speckled all over with the pitchings of
flies. XIV; And next a foundered staggered old
thing – covered with boils, rather agonized and
Heidegger heavy looking as if it might leap for the sky. No
wonder – Merrylegs has his teeth in his hind
quarters. But, my goodness, I believe it's the
horse we started out with, only, since we saw it
last it may have changed a bit you see what with
the merry-go-round going around you see.

When you're on it you don't notice this phenomenon but by that time you're a clown enjoying your pastime:[1] right now we are learneds and we are enjoying the puzzle of the Ferris wheel. As the baskets come round you see that this one is like a whole landscape suspended from two chains with (a) agricultural types dancing about a factory chimney (b) out of a bush wildly excited louts chase wild man dressed up in a skin of thick green painted leaves.

Basket Two contains (a) bonfire (b) men and women dancing about this (c) changing into a wheel which is dipped in pitch, set afire and set whirling like a huge sunflower down the green mountain (d) this wheel gets smaller but pretty soon it's up on top of the hill again as big as ever (e) look close and you can still see the men and women dancing around like seeds forming in the fire blossoms.

What does the third basket contain? Answer: (a) a circle of reapers in a field of deadripe wheat who are rapidly coming closer together in their circle until in the last knot of uncut grain a furious bird hisses up, sometimes a goose, a cat, a pig, even a little man (b) the bird escapes underneath the reapers' legs who pursue him with their scythes, binders and threshing machines and kill him (c) then they eat him. But next year the bird will still be there in the last sheaf of grain.

Basket Four reveals an inverted spring world: (a) it's November (b) through the trees of this wood I see stags leaping up into the air with forests on their heads. Of course it is their spring for it's the rutting season. Our dancers have lit a bonfire and some are leaping through it. People come to the fire with faggots and march away eyes of flame polkadotting the dark forest farther and farther away thereafter.

On a snowy ground in Basket Five men and women have catscradles in their hands which they keep changing from hand to hand into various patterns (a running man, a sunflower, an angry

---

1. A paraphrase of something Sir James Frazer says in *The Golden Bough*. The Ferris wheel turns through that book.

bird, a leaping deer, a wawling child): other dancers arrive beating drums, frying pans, sieves, kettles, their own heads until the stars fade, the snow disappears and out of the ground push the green claws & yellow horns and red tongues of a bonfire.

The next basket shows a happy child surrounded by men in wolf masks. A green wreath on his head, he is shaking a noisemaker and a rattle in his hands; on a pebble in front of him there is propped up a mirror, a present from his stepmother.

And the last basket contains the Sun and the Moon themselves with fat round bodies and faces beaming. The Moon has a dozen or so gray hounddogs in her arms and her lap: these are the ragged clouds she hunts with on stormy nights. Between her left hand & his right hand extends a web or catscradle of the tides and winds, rivers, fountains and whirlwinds which these two are continually changing into other patterns. The Moon looks domestic here; as a matter of fact, she is continually escaping from the Sun and her wanderings are recorded in spiral tattoo marks upon his left arm. By consulting these he knows where she has got to in her wanderings and when he will next be able to meet her face to face, he in the East and she in the West. In his left hand he holds a cage with a bird in it which represents the times they meet: like a falcon this bird is often sent out to search for her. This cage resembles a lantern.

THE CATERPILLAR RIDE

Goes round and opens up its dusky dusty top: infants look out hardening and changing into old men & women; the brown hood closes down, goes round, opens up, young children looking out and so on.

THE SIDESHOWS

Thunder, thunder & deal out light, darkness, Heaven-shell, Earth, Sea, plants, Sun & Moon, fishes, birds (whirr!) animals (grr!) and man and then all history with its gaudy banners stretches out down a lane in front of you: the banners glazed with the streaming rain although it could just be lice in the crotch and armpits and hair of creation. The first bunch of sideshow tents – after the exhibit of a huge whale on blocks of salt[1] which literally stinks to high heaven – are black. Inside you will see a dancing bear, a girl with Russell's viper, a talking crow with a split tongue that can read your hand, Siamese twins, a Cyclops, a four legs, a three arms, a no legs, a notable criminal pickled in a glass case on display. The second bunch are white tents: banners promise you the daughter of Chief White Man; she is a tremendous bearded fat woman the size of Mars' biggest moon at least; a dozen girls who take their clothes off, a man throwing a cloud of knives at a girl. In the yellow tents – shooting galleries, hooptoss, wheels of Fortune, a waxwork show with a torture chamber containing the Seven Steps to Heaven.

The last red tents contain a man in a sphere on a motorcycle, stilt walkers, fire eaters, sword swallowers, a talking pelican, a tremendous eagle, a man who gets in and out of a suitcase, and last of all the Grotto of the Beautiful Hermaphrodite.

THE DRUNKEN PREACHER

Lo, it was the last supper, I leader from gutter
Tell you tall and short tinkery folks gathered.
What did those white souls eat while their Lord talked:
I don't know indeed I don't, maybe sandwiches.
And He said haughtily head up to the twelve,
'I'll ask you assafoetidae again I will,
Isn't there one, one disciple with the spunk to betray me?'
They all fumbled their food, fed themselves slowly.
'Otherwise you see all my work ought in value is.'
'I will,' quavered weakly woefully poor Judas,
Runty little redhaired man runaway parents from him.
'I'll go through with ghoulish Holy Ghost necessary job.'
Even then at the end of it elder tree saw he.
His death, his Lord's death held him at Lord's supper.

---

1. A whale was exhibited in this way throughout Ontario some time during the thirties.

So you've all certainly betrayed him so you've done
Something for him by my bottle faith fiddle de dee you have.

Threshing machine still threshes throat-drying chaff;
Sun with its sperm belt spangles against cog moon,
Fat horses at farm fetch the wheel round & round,
In the rain-mud runcible 'aroint thee' bubbling.
They haul out from high loft, fork handfuls of pea straw
Beneath bashing horsehooves.
Little babe loudly screams, last thunder of year.

October

ARGUMENT: *Branwell sings a very autumnal song; he has never recovered from the disastrous affair with Dorcas. His nettle suit has turned brown & dry with age.*

[RAYMOND BRANWELL]

Sing to us for the frost
   Is closing the pond,
The elms their leaves have lost
And the singing birds have gone.

BRANWELL

What can I sing to you?
   I have a song
Perhaps it will do,
I found it at the Fair.

GREEN grove walk toward me,
   Around me with
      That which
Trembles heartsmith.

Currant tinkle bobbob
   Pheasant leap whir
      Squirrel
A pink mushroom, sir!

Little missy white violets
   Squirrel corn
      Bloodroots
Bossy lost her horn.

As yet not boxes
   Gallows
      Legs, pulpits
Of trees windblows.

Hollow tree tuwhoos
   Come here
      Mousie
And robin redbreast dear.

Far away red faraway
   Red as fire
      A fox
Flash and transpire.

I met a green woman:
Her feet were paths
Her eyes were bunchberries
Her arms elm laths
Her tongue a mushroom
Her teeth white violets
Her nose an owl feather,
Her mouth like cressets.

Did I touch her?
   Vanished.
      Twang!
Garnisheed

All pulse-wage since
   And this place
Holds my heart in a bottle
   of pathpace.

RAYMOND

This song is like the grapes now
   Black in the arbours of fences,

Wild apples from their lane bough
    Savage and sweet to the senses.

Nailed and studded are the quietnesses
    With wrinkled dark butternuts,
Prickly beechnuts of brown darknesses,
    Ripe burs' pinch and hook and clutch.

The shorter sun sets farther south,
    The foxes are about now,
The wind whistles with a narrow mouth,
Up to the gooseshed we had better go.

November

ARGUMENT: *Four birds discuss the calendar. Mopsus has certainly come a long way from the detachment & 'calm canals' he mentioned at first.*

[OOKPIK STARLING WILDGOOSE MOPSUS]

Birdies, can there be any doubt
My master, Winter, turns the wheel,
　The Miller whom none love.
I at the spindle pole have been
And through the swarming shuddering snow
　Seen at work the God of Death;
Winter and Death turn all the world,
Man and continents come apart
　Like skin from flesh from bone.
The world was planned in cold arithmetic,
Numbers flapping like vultures fast & thick
Down and around my merry Master Zero
Like birds of prey about a stone dead hero.

STARLING

The year begins when it grows warm;
Then I once more do mate and chirp
　And fly out from the town.
It is not year or time at all
When all there's eatable is dung
　And all is frozen round.
Give me the eaves of a steam laundry
Where I dream of upperworld spring
　Above this grave of cold.
Once I lived in a place of sun,
I wish I knew how there to run,

Migrationless I debris am
Yet know the world begins with warm.

WILDGOOSE

My wings tell me that September[1]
Shall the year's beginning be;
    Up those wide rungs I climb
And fly a vigorous sabbath south
And find no winter in my year
    But live a summer seesaw;
Two summers like a figure eight
Two wings like tables of the law
    Are my four seasons.
The wobbling earth with its Goliath snows
I steady and defeat with feathered blows.
The year begins when death and chaos sprout
And I must with a new world beat them out.

1. The Jews begin their year in September.

MOPSUS

A sun, a moon, a crowd of stars,
A calendar nor clock is he
    By whom I start my year.
He is most like a sun for he
Makes his beholders into suns,
    Shadowless and timeless.
At the winter sunstill some say
He dared be born; on darkest day
    A babe of seven hours
He crushed the four proud and great directions
Into the four corners of his small cradle.
He made it what time of year he pleased, changed
Snow into grass and gave to all such powers.

December

ARGUMENT: *Most of the geese are executed. Those geese to be saved are marked off with marking rings on their legs. Branwell's is taken from him by George, but Effie willingly gives hers up. She prefers to help Branwell face the block & also to go with him into the new dimension she hopes awaits them after death. We leave the goosehouse, the farmhouse and finally enter our own world again.*

Day of wrath and terror came now!
Chop chop chop chop chop
The farmers killed their geese for Christmas market.
Each day Peter came and took a dozen
Held their feet with one hand and with other
Brought down the axe that severs dreading heart
From dreading mind; Mopsus went first
And suffered stubbornly running about
The yard for minutes without his head.
Some said, 'Care for my little mouse,' and some
Said what a small slender neck it was;
Others, 'The gods themselves weep o'er such dooms,'
Or, 'Goose Grease! what crimes are done in thy name.'
The cats and dogs ran away with their heads,
Betty and Ann then plucked off their feathers,
Stoppered their necks with brown paper and tied
Their legs together ready for market stall.
Betty chose Branwell and Dorcas, Effie, Valancy
And Old Keziah to keep the race alive.

GEORGE

Help! Help! He's choosing those without the rings.
They put the rings on you to mark you off.
Give me your ring! Why bother saving you?

Ow! These nettles sting. I'm the buck
That'll keep the race alive for them.

BRANWELL

Well, what do I do now? Wait for Peter I guess.
I'd hardly realized what the rings were for.

EFFIE

Who could be glad to be left alive, who could
Cling to this cramped stupid goosehouse world.
For 'Death's the green pathway' to the fields of Life
'Die would we daily once it to expert.'
Help me off with this pink marking ring.
Fanny, see if it will fit your leg.
Who knows, at the very least we become men
When we die. Take off the suit of nettles
Of our selves. Here, Branwell, listen to the ring
You think might save your life. What does it sound like?

BRANWELL

It's the merry-go-round at the fair
Or the Ferris wheel far far far away.

EFFIE

Life inside of that is a crazed prison
Of despair. You can't possibly want it.

BRANWELL

I can't help it, I'm afraid, I want the ring.
I can't see a path that leads between one's
Head & one's body.

When you are changed then
One arm may always remain a goose wing.

On Christmas Day at farmhouse they ate dinner,
Stuffing themselves with two roast geese at least
And picking their teeth with thin bone from drumsticks
They slept that night on fatter featherticks,
Mother Holl shook down feathers from the sky.

A pail of time tipped back into another pail,
Leftover fly from summer buzzing on ceiling,
A feather gleamed upon Peter's wrist and Ann
Swept the top of the stove with a goosewing.

Drowning in the waterflames of Love
They lay in the straw with it snowing in the loft window.

Keziah quite an old goose gray as the winter twilight in a city
Clambered up into her nest to begin laying.
She was like
Coming out of the William Avenue Public Library,
People flowing up Main Street,[1] sadly,
Each person a gray feather, the streetlights like
All the possible eggs inside her and the streetcar an orange beak coming toward you.

---

1. Winnipeg.